Between the stars where you are lost

poems by

Mary Christine Kane

Finishing Line Press
Georgetown, Kentucky

Between the stars where you are lost

Copyright © 2019 by Mary Christine Kane
ISBN 978-1-63534-953-5 First Edition
All rights reserved under International and Pan-American Copyright Conventions. No part of this book may be reproduced in any manner whatsoever without written permission from the publisher, except in the case of brief quotations embodied in critical articles and reviews.

ACKNOWLEDGMENTS

Thank you to the editors of the following publications, in which these poems originally appeared:

Vermillion Literary Project magazine: "The best years"
Bluestem: "My mother mowing the lawn at twilight"
Parks and Points: "Winter, Lake Erie, New York"
Portage Magazine: "Toad love"
Talking Stick: "The plain things"

So many people have influenced this collection—with prompts, editing, steering me back to the path and other ways I could never measure. For your creative, editorial and/or emotional support, thank you Deborah Keenan, Erica Skog, Hallie Wiederholt, Ruth Taylor, the Hamline Alumni Poetry Book Club, Jim Moore, Renita Picotte, and Paige Riehl. And of course, mom and dad, my champions.

A special thanks to Susan Solomon for the gorgeous and dreamy cover artwork. More of her beautiful work can be found at www.instagram.com/solomon.painter.

Publisher: Leah Maines
Editor: Christen Kincaid
Cover Art: Susan Solomon, susansolomonpainter.com
Author Photo: Jenna Lipscomb
Cover Design: Elizabeth Maines McCleavy

Printed in the USA on acid-free paper.
Order online: www.finishinglinepress.com
also available on amazon.com

Author inquiries and mail orders:
Finishing Line Press
P. O. Box 1626
Georgetown, Kentucky 40324
U. S. A.

Table of Contents

The best years 1

When Ricky stayed with us 2

To the collector 3

Dear God of My Childhood, ... 4

My mother mowing the lawn at twilight 6

Your voice 7

Winter *Lake Erie, New York* 8

Toad love 9

On the color red 10

To the girl in the pew 11

To anger rising up 12

Andre 13

There is no meantime 15

50 questions for any god who will listen,
    once my body perishes 16

The plain things 18

Summer *Lake Erie, New York* 19

To the curtains hanging still, slightly dirty,
    slightly crooked 20

Reading the world 21

Notes 22

The best years

In sequestered afternoons,
children sit in basements
with televisions and potato chips
dazing
until their heads swell like balloons
and lips plump with salt.

They do not get around to dreaming
but follow the arms of the wall clock
ticking closer to mom, dad
a warm dinner to temper
hungry bellies.
They are told, *any minute now.*

They are told, *these are the best years,*
a puzzle they will consider later,
while counting minutes between Mississippis
while counting sheep over wooden fences
while counting how many
of their best years are left.

When Ricky stayed with us

All in all you were all just bricks in the wall.
Pink Floyd

It was ordinary how the three of us were born to loving mothers and found ourselves in Tonawanda, a place named by the Tuscarora, meaning "confluent stream," a naming which became tragic when it was the blood from many skins flowing together.

On the way to the hospital Ricky's mom dropped him at our house, so she could heal her fleshy, bloody body from the wounds of Ricky's dad, a man we knew from a distance and were confused about why he was married to Ricky's mom, who looked like a grandma, not knowing that beating a person is like beating a ball of dough: it resists, dents, hollows, then toughens.

Ricky brought the new Pink Floyd 45, the likes of which we had never heard before. We set the needle in the groove and watched as Ricky sang and danced his skinny white welted ass around our scratchy sofas and cat-clawed drapes. *We don't need no thought control.*

My brother and I joined, *leave them kids alone!* We flailed and kicked to that sharpness that resisted easy movement, the room barely big enough for us. *Would thrash them within inches of their lives.*

I'm not sure how long Ricky stayed or when they disappeared. I know he and my brother raced their pine derby cars in boy scouts that year and it was their mothers who watched.

I don't need no arms around me. Don't think I need anything at all.

To the collector

A small pile of rings, bought from toy machines
for the thrill of placing the quarter in the slot
where it fits just right,
the click click click as she turns the silver handle
with her hand that is soft
as a pillow,
and listens, breath held
quiet as a cloud,
as the bubble drops
down the tunnel
to the
the dispenser
where her palm waits.

She pulls apart the plastic container
and finds either joy
or disappointment.
The plastic jewels
are worn for special occasions
and must be removed before
going potty, as is the house rule
on account of how loose
they are and prone to dangling
and mother does not want
to fish any more out of the bowl.

There is always a need for another
quarter.

Dear God of My Childhood,

I am sorry for the delay.
The directions misled.
They said, *Look into the eyes of others.*
Look deep into your own heart.
I took this seriously.

I saw that some are always crying a little,
their crying, a companion.
I saw when some smile
it is like a forklift lifting their mouths.
Their eyes remain still and dark like parking lots.
I saw that some are cotton
and can be lifted in a moment
into dance, laughter, generosity.
Others want to be near them.
They become idols.
I did not know which somes were you.

They said you are in all things.

I looked deep
and saw children in the grass
flushed cheeks, hair shining.
Rolling down an uncle's hill
arms tucked, legs crossed
trying to miss the pine tree
that Uncle Tony said got its lump when cousin Karen hit it.
We giggled and rolled, rolled and giggled.

I saw grandma
light up and scurry toward me,
slippers scraping linoleum.
She grabs my cheeks and kisses me
as if I were the best thing ever created.
Her mole brushed my cheek.
I didn't mind.
I saw a lot of us Lord—I didn't know where you were.

They said look for signs.
There were always signs:
The rosaries in grandma's drawers,
the pictures of your son in every bedroom.
The paramedic who told me she believed in you
while she took my pulse as we raced to the hospital.
The friend who died before we were ready,
after he had quit drinking, smoking, running from you.
The songs they told me that were laced with evil
(if you could play them backwards, they said,
you'd hear).
The people dying on tv.
The slums I saw from my tourist bus.

They said God is everywhere,
except where he is not.

I hope I am your child.
I hope there is a heaven
with a cove full of deeply green
trees that opens to a meadow
with rolling hills and singing birds
and grandmothers waiting for their grandchildren.
I hope what we long for
becomes eternally true.

But in this world
my mind is much too small
for you.

My mother mowing the lawn at twilight

She made sweet, curved lines, following
paths of sidewalk
around maple roots and strawberry vines.
Fresh cuts fell on concrete.
We followed with rakes and trash bags.

But she had started too late, again,
forecast for rain, baths to be drawn.
We tense, as if this were the last inning.
We want us to win.

Dark settled into her baby-fine hair
sank deep into chocolate eyes
landed on slim shoulders
rounded into column
of torso
slipped into thin,
strong
legs.

Grass-stained tennies kept on
intermittedly lit by street lights
until the dark shut us down,
red turning to granite.

Later we would call for her
claiming thirst, fear of dark.
She brought hurried kisses.

The light from the kitchen seeped under our doors.
Then rings and whispers.
We strained to hear
who it was
and how he might change things.

Your voice

When someone called
you said *hello*
but it sounded like
yellow.
When we didn't mind you
you yelled like
a vibrating
bird.
I would have liked to have heard
the girlish giggle
from your first
life.
Your
trembling
I do.

Winter

Lake Erie, New York

The uncles
have been out on the ice again.
They bring home trout
which grandma will bread and fry.
Their bodies turn the kitchen cold.
We breathe in chill.

Toad love

She ran into the kitchen
muddy feet, tender heart
toad cupped in tiny hands

dropped it in a tub
big enough for cottage cheese
too small for survival.

It tucked its tiny feet inside itself
a baby missing its womb,
I looked away.

She ran for twigs
grass, comfort
dinner ants

arranged the container
quickly and skillfully
and announced, *It can't escape.*

Later, I thought of you and you
and you
and then me and then us

how we've been removed
from the garden
how we've been replanted inside.

I cannot stand to see the toad in the tub.

We let her keep it
because she thinks it knows her heart
and this seems like something.

On the color red

When you see red
it does not mean you are angry,
only that you are full.
Blood pouring with placenta
tricycle winding its way to her house
peonies bursting beside the open doorway
a kitchen of tomato perfume
sauce drips on your white shirt
sleep beside the whirring fan.
She comes with Calamine
calming every itchy bump.

To the girl in the pew

To aloneness, not solitude.
Running for the red ball
no one is behind you.

To longing, not to wanting
to hoping, which is not dreaming
to wondering, which is not knowing.

To picking the white blossom off the tree
and running up to give it to a lady,
to hoping her kiss feels like a mommy's.

To let's imagine all the people in church have no mommies now.
To let's play mommy is dead on the way home.
You go first.

To anger rising up

When will you know what you are?
You, incited one
caught in your tunnel
not knowing whether to explode
like flame on tinder
or inch back
like a scolded lion.
In a striking display
you, passionate heart
unsure whether you are born
of the rough and pure
energy of dance
or the sourness of a sin
kept too long a secret.
Are you brilliant from your core?
Are you painted refuse?
When will you know what you are?

Andre

> *I might not have known his voice*
> *And he would have known mine*
> *As one-too-many wrong numbers.*
>   Gerald Barrax

For a time, other men auditioned
as husband,
father.
They brought candy,
canned jokes.
They chewed with their mouths open,
forgot to say *please,*
thank you.

She started smelling like gardenias
and wearing shiny things.

There was the man from
community ed
who called too much.
The one from the football game
who said *darlin'.*
The guy from work,
who had already dated Terese
with *perfect hair*
no kids
a different outfit for every day of the month.

And then, Andre, a dutchman.
Tall, gangly—he stooped over to give her hugs.
His rounded back made him fit better
in the bright yellow Volkswagen
which he took them in to do doughnuts
in snowy parking lots
on the way to Chinese and pancake dinners.

Everyone gained weight
and watched him perform.
Night after night he whipped up fun.

They did not mention love
or take a portrait:
the awkward four of them
for placing atop a fireplace.
One day the yellow car
stopped appearing.

Twenty years later,
David looked him up.
Andre shared pictures:
his wife, children.
They ate dinner,
said goodbye.

There is no meantime

Before we become shadows
let's hear the chime of the spoon
as we mix the berries.
Let's be curious how the purples and
reds will assemble in our
bone-white bowl.
Let's follow the notes of the music
into our bones; let's hold them there.
Let's be held; let's not say love is fleeting.
Let's feel the leaves shake the rain from its tree.
Let's watch the bucket fill.

50 questions for any god who will listen, once my body perishes

1. If he hadn't called.
2. If I had better known the geography of the world.
3. If I could have sorted out the differences between loves.
4. If I had found more things funny.
5. If I'd been taller.
6. If I had said *yes* more readily, even though I meant, *I am not sure*, just because it was a thing for him to ask.
7. If I were still in the kitchen on Parkhurst, wrapped in the seafoam robe choosing my next frosted donut.
8. If I had eaten fewer frosted donuts.
9. If I had had the stomach for practicing medicine.
10. If I had been less sentimental.
11. If, for me, it hadn't so often started with a him.
12. If I had known how it would end.
13. If the percent of wounded people had been lower.
14. If the water had decided to recede and not return.
15. If I had understood earlier there was no secret.
16. If I had yearned less for truth.
17. If capitalism hadn't destroyed so many words.
18. If I had lived *up to my potential*, as they say.
19. If my face hadn't gotten stuck in a ten-year frown, which my mother had warned me about.
20. If I had understood what the trees had whispered to me.
21. If I had not just mouthed the hymns.
22. If I learned sooner that no one was watching, except for the people I had not considered.
23. If I had never felt the soft, warm belly of a puppy.
24. If I had been born two hundred years earlier.
25. If I had gotten married the first time I said I would.
26. If no one had taught me to read.
27. If my beloved brother and I had not had a pebble stuck between us.
28. If the birds had put a moratorium on singing.
29. If I had never practiced lying.
30. If I had stayed quiet for the lamenting pause.

31. If I had been less afraid of a thousand things.
32. If I had so *no* more readily, because I *knew*.
33. If I had loved amputees half as much as broken branches, which I cradled and replanted in my dreams.
34. If I had never seen an unmasked man.
35. If I had understood earlier how everything important must be done alone.
36. If I had been more daring.
37. If we had not traded wilderness for this brand of *abundance*.
38. If we had had a few more years on the prairie, following falcons.
39. If that god had only added seven protons to oxygen.
40. If the rocks had decided to dissolve more dramatically.
41. If my parents had been rich enough to worry I would be stolen for ransom.
42. If I had been more reckless, then less reckless.
43. If I were any other color.
44. If I had never craved more than I was given.
45. If I had been born on the other side of the world, my belly swollen with scarcity—the faraway story my mother had told us about over dinner.
46. If I had understood that when you said *I don't want to*, you also meant *I don't know how*.
47. If the boat with my ancestors had never left the harbor.
48. If my drunkenness had not been the quarrelsome sort.
49. If gluttony had remained a sin.
50. If I could visit my grandmother when she was a girl and comb her silky hair.

The plain things

Today I wanted
just a picture of you
with your squat dog
in that bright orange sweater
you crocheted for her
so her little white body
wouldn't get lost
in piles of
Buffalo snow.

I remembered,
it is the plain things
we will long for:

The bowl with the gold-scalloped edges
pastel flowers at bottom
ladled full of soup.
Your purse stocked with gum, crackers,
rosaries.

I wanted just a picture,
you planting tomatoes
in that thin strip of dirt lining your driveway,
moss kerchief fluttering.
You stirring sauce
with the burnt-edged wooden spoon.
You crocheting in the parlor,
curious dog by your feet.
You scurrying to the door
fuzzy slippers scraping linoleum
to welcome us in.

Summer

Lake Erie, New York

Grandpa has bought new beach robes, white terry stitched with gold. I think this makes us look rich. I feel so fancy I comb my hair 50 extra times.

David and I watch her waves come from Canada. We see the skyline and dream of swimming to that other world.

The lake is full of glass. She smoothes their sharp edges into curves. We comb for hours, stepping over fish bones to uncover jewels of emerald, cobalt, amber.

Grandpa lifts us on his shoulders and tosses us in. His black-rimmed glasses catch glints of sun; we try to not get them wet.

One year I throw away a drawer-full of glass, thinking it silly.

I wish I had that terry robe. I long for a piece of Erie glass.

To the curtains hanging still, slightly dirty, slightly crooked

Lets certain
light in
and through.

In the part
between the panels,
is where the girl looks
for hours.

Reading the world

I am the waves that reach for you,
I am the waving plants of the sea.

I am fire that breathes and gusts
wafting cinder, drinking flame—

peach-blue of morning
when the sky blooms over a sleeping landscape
No one is a stranger here.

Curves forming on bark for the first time:
white heart.

Chill of night
that frosted the grass.

The glass you dream of,
the one that doesn't break, you keep looking through.

The space between the stars
where you are lost.

Rain that soaks to bone
thunder calling you home.

I am open, green—
I spill over the earth with living.

Notes

The epigraph and italicized text in "When Ricky stayed with us" is from Pink Floyd's "Another Brick in the Wall—Part 2." The Wall, Capitol Records, 1979

The epigraph in "Andre" is from Gerald Barrax's poem "Last Letter," which appears in *Every Shut Eye Ain't Asleep*.

Born in Texas, **Mary Christine Kane** grew up in Western New York and has lived in Minneapolis most of her adult life. She works in marketing and is a volunteer for the arts and animal rescue. Her poetry and nonfiction has appeared in journals and anthologies including *Bluestem; The Buffalo Anthology, Right Here, Right Now; Ponder Review; Plainsongs* and others. This is her first collection.

www.ingramcontent.com/pod-product-compliance
Lightning Source LLC
LaVergne TN
LVHW041523070426
835507LV00012B/1779